T0096901

Cake Pops!

Cake Pops!

25 BITE-SIZED SWEET TREATS

HANNAH MILES

LORENZ BOOKS

This edition is published by
Lorenz Books, an imprint of
Anness Publishing Ltd
108 Great Russell Street
London WC1B 3NA

info@anness.com

www.lorenzbooks.com
www.annesspublishing.com

If you like the images in this book
and would like to investigate using
them for publishing, promotions or
advertising, please visit our website
www.practicalpictures.com for
more information.

© Anness Publishing Ltd 2015

All rights reserved. No part of this
publication may be reproduced,
stored in a retrieval system, or
transmitted in any way or by any
means, electronic, mechanical,
photocopying, recording or otherwise,
without the prior written permission
of the copyright holder.

A CIP catalogue record for this book is
available from the British Library.

Publisher: Joanna Lorenz
Editor: Kate Eddison, Helen Sudell
Photographer: Nicki Dowey
Food Stylist: Aya Nishimura
Prop Stylist: Wei Tang
Designer: Lisa Tai
Production Controller: Pirong Wang

COOK'S NOTES

- Bracketed terms are intended for American readers.
- For all recipes, quantities are given in both metric and imperial measures and,
  where appropriate, in standard cups and spoons. Follow one set of measures,
  but not a mixture, because they are not interchangeable.
- Standard spoon and cup measures are level. 1 tsp = 5ml, 1 tbsp = 15ml,
  1 cup = 250ml/8fl oz.
- Australian standard tablespoons are 20ml. Australian readers should use 3 tsp in
  place of 1 tbsp for measuring small quantities.
- American pints are 16fl oz/2 cups. American readers should use 20fl oz/2.5 cups
  in place of 1 pint when measuring liquids.
- Electric oven temperatures in this book are for conventional ovens. When using a fan
  oven, the temperature will probably need to be reduced by about 10–20°C/20–40°F.
  Since ovens vary, you should check with your manufacturer's instruction book
  for guidance.
- The nutritional analysis given for each recipe, unless otherwise stated, is calculated
  per portion (i.e. serving or item). If the recipe gives a range, such as Serves 4–6, then
  the nutritional analysis will be for the smaller size, i.e. 6 servings. The analysis does
  not include optional ingredients, such as salt added to taste.
- Medium (US large) eggs are used unless otherwise stated.

PUBLISHER'S NOTE

Although the advice and information in this book are believed to be accurate and
true at the time of going to press, neither the authors nor the publisher can accept
any legal responsibility or liability for any errors or omissions that may have been
made nor for any inaccuracies nor for any loss, harm or injury that comes about
from following instructions or advice in this book.

Previously published as part of a larger volume, *Cake Pops*.

Contents

Introduction 6

Cake Pop Equipment 8

Tips and Techniques 10

Cake Pop Recipes 12

Classic Cake Pops 14

Cookie Pops 26

Party Pops 32

Rich & Indulgent Pops 46

Holiday Pops 54

Index 64

Introduction

Welcome to the wonderful world of pops – cake pops, cookie pops and other yummy treats on sticks. From the classic truffle-style cake pops and buttery crumble cakes to crisp meringues and chewy cookie pops, there is a favourite in this book for everyone.

What is a cake pop?

The classic cake pop is a delicious ball of sponge truffle which can be flavoured and coloured in many different ways, served on sticks and decorated with yummy chocolate or ganache. They can also be crafted into fun characters, such as bumble bees or frogs that will delight young children at a birthday party. In this book, the idea of cake pops has been expanded to include beautiful, mini versions of popular cakes, which are intricately embellished and served on sticks. There is also a selection of irresistible cookie pops, which never fail to please with young and old alike.

Pops for all occasions

Cake pops should, generally, be just one mouthful so that they are easy to eat and your fingers do not get sticky. They are ideal for serving at parties as a sweet canapé, when people like to keep their hands free. They offer great opportunities for some 'wow factor' presentation with creative and dainty decoration. Dusted with edible glitter or topped with gold leaf, your cake pops will literally twinkle and are sure to offer a talking point at any gathering. Let your imagination run wild when decorating – the more elaborate the designs, the more you will be delighted with the results.

Displaying cake pops

There are many ways of serving cookie and cake pops. Cookie pops can be laid flat on platters or serving trays. Cake pops can be more challenging to display, though sufficient cake pop stands are now available to buy in specialist cake shops and online. If you are serving cake pops on long thin skewers, you can insert the skewers into polystyrene (Styrofoam) blocks. Or why not display them in vases or tall

Above: Cake pops are not just for children. There is a great selection of sophisticated recipes for adult palates in this book.

Above: Pops can be shaped and decorated in an endless variety of ways to appeal to all ages.

glasses? If you serve pops regularly, you can make a display rack by drilling small holes into a wooden display board. A simple method is to serve the pops on a serving plate or cake stand with the sticks pointing upwards. This is especially useful for heavier pops.

Some cake pops need to be served very soon after being assembled on sticks as the weight of the cake will cause the pops to slip down the sticks if left for too long. The best options to prevent them slipping are either to keep them in the refrigerator until just before serving or, alternatively, to fix a mini marshmallow on to the skewers below the cakes, which will act as a stopper and prevent the cakes from slipping down the sticks.

Take particular care when choosing sticks for cake pops given to children – do not use sharp, pointy skewers, and make sure you collect all the sticks up as soon as the pops have been eaten so that they do not become a safety hazard.

Be creative with cake pops

Once you have grasped the basic concept of the classic ball-shaped, truffle-style cake pop, you will easily be able to experiment with other flavour combinations and ideas for decorations. If you are short of time, you can substitute ready-made cake into the recipes – store-bought ginger cake or lemon sponge work very well. You will need to use 200g/7 oz of ready-made cake as a substitute for any of the classic cake pop recipes in this book.

Above: There is a lot of fun to be had in making and decorating a special batch of fabulous cake pops for a children's birthday party.

Decorating your cake pops

One of the nicest things about making pops is the wide variety of decorating options. White chocolate blended with a few drops of food colouring will make pretty, pastel pops. Food colouring gels give a strong shade and blend well with chocolate, but pastes and powders also work well.

For decoration, you can use sugar sprinkles or sugar sand. Applied to melted chocolate or icing while still wet, they will attach firmly when the icing or chocolate sets. Edible lustre spray can be used, together with edible glitter and gold leaf, all of which are available from cake decorating shops. These are lovely for an evening party as they really twinkle under lights.

Cake Pop Equipment

You will need a relatively small amount of baking equipment to make the recipes in this book, and you will probably have most of it already in your own kitchen. Although some items involve an initial cost, they really do make baking easier and are a worthwhile investment.

Tins (pans) Many different tins can be used to make pops. It is worth investing in good quality tins that will not rust or distort over time. Loose-bottomed tins have a base that can be lifted out, making it easy to remove the cake. If you do not have the tin called for in a recipe you can use a similar-sized tin, but be aware that the cooking time may need to be adjusted.

Silicone cake moulds There is a large variety of silicone moulds

Above: An electric whisk makes beating cake mixtures an easy task.

available. They can be baked in the oven and cakes literally pop out of them when cooked. They come in decorative patterns and shapes, and are ideal for making mini cakes. If you do not have the mould required for a recipe, you can bake the cake in a square cake tin and then cut to the size or shape needed.

Mixers and whisks It is useful to have a stand mixer for some of the recipes in this book. While balloon whisks are good for recipes that do not need much whipping, whisking cake mixtures and cream is much faster using an electric hand whisk or an electric stand mixer.

Sieve (strainer) Essential for sifting flour, cocoa powder and icing (confectioners') sugar, a sieve is an indispensable piece of equipment.

Wire rack Once cookies and cakes are baked, you need to cool them on a wire rack. If they stay in the hot tin or on the hot baking sheet, they can overcook. Let cakes and cookies cool in the tin (pan) or on the baking sheet for a few minutes before releasing them. This will reduce the chance of them breaking as you transfer them to the wire rack.

Baking parchment and silicone mats A non-stick paper, baking parchment is used to line cake

Above: A piping bag and a range of nozzles are essential decorating tools.

Above: A sugar thermometer is used to make a few recipes in this book, such as meringues.

tins (pans) and baking sheets. If you bake regularly, you may wish to consider investing in silicone mats. These are thick mats on which you can cook without greasing. Nothing sticks to them so they are ideal for baking cookies and meringues.

Weighing scales Baking is a scientific process, and it is important that ingredients are weighed and measured carefully for best results. For the most accurate quantities use electronic weighing scales.

Sugar thermometer This is essential when working with hot liquids where the temperature reached is critical for the recipe, such as marshmallows.

Blow torch A chef's blow torch can be used to caramelize sugar and meringue. If you do not have one, it is possible in some recipes to use a hot grill (broiler) instead.

Chocolate dipping fork This tool enables you to dip truffle centres into melted chocolate or ganache to ensure that the whole truffle is coated. If you do not have one, you can achieve similar results by using a fork.

Piping (pastry) bag and nozzles For effective and neat decoration when icing a cake, best results are achieved when using a piping bag with nozzle attachments. Nozzles come in many different shapes and sizes, allowing you to be wonderfully creative when decorating. The best way to learn how to use a piping bag and nozzle is to make a large batch of buttercream or royal icing, and pipe different shapes using each nozzle to see what results you can achieve. Piping bags are available in many forms – waterproof fabric bags that can be reused repeatedly, or

Above: You can buy all sorts of sticks and skewers, and can colour plain sticks with food colouring.

disposable plastic bags. If you are icing using several different colours it is easiest to use disposable bags.

Pastry (cookie) cutters These come in all sorts of shapes and sizes, and are needed for cutting out cookies.

Skewers and sticks A wide variety of skewers and sticks is available in shops and online. When serving to children you need to remove any sharp points so that they don't cause injury. Check the sticks are appropriate for food use, especially if they are coloured. If you are baking the stick in the oven, you need to make sure the stick is suitable for baking at high temperatures.

Tips and Techniques

Once you have mastered the basic skills and techniques for successful baking you will be able to create beautiful cake and cookie pops at home. There are a few techniques that will come up time and time again in the recipes, so it is worth getting to grips with them.

Melting chocolate

Ensure that all the equipment you use is dry, as water can affect the melting properties of chocolate. Break the chocolate into pieces and place in a heatproof bowl. If you are making chocolate ganache, you add the butter and cream to the bowl at this stage. Place the bowl over a small pan of simmering water, ensuring that the bottom of the bowl does not touch the water. Gently simmer until the chocolate has melted. Take care when handling the bowl as it will be hot.

Alternatively to melt chocolate in a microwave, place the chocolate (and cream and butter, if you are making a ganache) in a microwave-proof bowl and microwave on full power for 1–1½ minutes until the chocolate has melted, stopping every 10–20 seconds to stir the chocolate so that it doesn't burn.

Preparing buttercream

To make buttercream, sift 225g/8oz/2 cups icing (confectioners') sugar into a large mixing bowl and add 125g/4¼oz/½ cup of butter. The butter must be very soft otherwise you will end up with lumps. Add 15ml/1 tbsp milk and a little vanilla extract, and whisk using an electric hand whisk or in an electric stand mixer for 2–3 minutes until the mixture is very light, adding a little more milk if it is too dry. Spoon into a piping (pastry) bag fitted with a suitable nozzle, and you are ready to start decorating.

Whipping to 'peaks'

Creating whipped peaks is easiest in an electric stand mixer or using an electric hand whisk; it can be done with a balloon whisk, but it takes a long time. Place the

Above: Chocolate can be melted over a pan of simmering water or, for speed, in a microwave.

Above: Cream whipped to 'stiff peaks' should hold its shape when lifted up on the whisk.

Shaping and decorating classic cake pops

The classic cake pop balls are simple to make, and they provide a great base for creative decorations.

1 To prepare the cake pops, make the cake in the recipe (or use ready-made sponge cake). Process the cake to crumbs. Mix in the recipe ingredients to moisten the crumbs to create a paste-like truffle mixture.

2 Take small pieces of the truffle mixture and form into your desired shape using your fingers. Place on a tray and chill in the freezer for 30 minutes. Once they are firm, press a stick or skewer into each one.

3 Dip into melted chocolate or ganache, making sure the whole truffle is coated. Decorate while the cake pop is still sticky, and then leave to set in a foam block. Store them in the refrigerator until ready to serve.

cream or egg whites in a clean, dry bowl and whisk until the cream or egg whites stand in peaks when you lift up the beaters.

For 'soft peaks', the mixture should hold its shape but just flop over slightly. For 'stiff peaks', the mixture should stand firm in peaks. When whipping cream, take care not to over-whip it, as the cream will separate.

Icing sugars

Different icing sugars are used in the recipes. Icing (confectioners') sugar is a very fine, powdered sugar that dissolves in water to produce a runny icing that sets. It can be coloured with food colouring. Instant royal icing sugar is icing sugar mixed with dried egg white (meringue powder). You can make royal icing by whisking 250g/9oz cups

sifted icing sugar with 1 egg white, lightly beaten, and 15ml/ 1 tbsp lemon juice for 3–5 minutes until it holds stiff peaks. Fondant (regal) icing sugar contains glucose and sets with a glossy finish. If you can't get hold of it, just use icing sugar instead. Ready-to-roll icing is a thick sugarpaste (fondant) that can be used to make decorations or to cover cakes.

Cake Pop Recipes

If you are fond of baking cakes but would love to create new tempting one-bite treats, then the recipes that follow are just what you need. Delight young children with a batch of colourful Honey Bee Pops or bright green Frog Pops; cause a stir at tea-time with Mini Cupcake Pops; and impress your dinner party guests with sophisticated Mocha Gold Leaf Pops. Whatever the occasion, these fun cake pop creations will not disappoint.

Mini Victoria Sponge Pops

The Victoria sponge is one of England's most popular teatime treats – light vanilla cakes sandwiched together with buttercream and jam, and dusted with icing sugar. These mini versions are perfect for serving with a pot of freshly brewed tea for an afternoon tea party.

Makes 10

50g/2oz/¼ cup butter, softened
50g/2oz/¼ cup caster
(superfine) sugar
1 egg
5ml/1 tsp vanilla extract
50g/2oz/½ cup self-raising
(self-rising) flour, sifted
5ml/1 tsp baking powder
10 lollipop sticks

For the buttercream and jam filling
100g/3¾oz/scant 1 cup icing
(confectioners') sugar,
plus extra for dusting
30g/1¼oz/2½ tbsp butter,
softened
30g/1¼oz/scant ¼ cup cream
cheese
5ml/1 tsp vanilla extract
a little milk, for mixing (optional)
60–75ml/4–5 tbsp good quality
strawberry jam

To decorate
10 tiny ribbons (optional)

1 Preheat the oven to 180°C/350°F/Gas 4. Grease a 10-cup straight-sided mini muffin tin (pan) or silicone mould. To make the cakes, cream the butter and sugar together until fluffy. Beat in the egg and vanilla extract.

2 Sift the flour and baking powder into the butter mixture, then fold in. Divide the cake mixture (batter) between the cups of the prepared tin or mould. Bake for 12–15 minutes, until the cakes spring back when gently pressed. Transfer to a wire rack to cool.

3 For the buttercream, sift the icing sugar into a bowl, add the butter, cream cheese and vanilla extract, and whisk together for 3 minutes, or until light and creamy, adding a little milk if necessary.

4 Cut each of the cakes in half horizontally. Using a piping (pastry) bag fitted with a small star-shaped nozzle, pipe the buttercream on to the bottom half of each cake. Using a teaspoon, add a little strawberry jam to each. Top with the other cake halves and dust with sifted icing sugar. Insert a lollipop stick into the top of each cake and tie a ribbon around it.

Energy 177kcal/742kJ; Protein 2g; Carbohydrate 24g, of which sugars 20g; Fat 9g, of which saturates 5g; Cholesterol 45mg; Calcium 33mg; Fibre 0.3g; Sodium 136mg.

Red Velvet Pops

Red velvet cake is an all-time American classic. Dainty cupcakes are coloured red and flavoured with cocoa to give them their distinctive look and taste. The lovely sharpness of the cream cheese icing perfectly complements the sweet sponge cake.

Makes 20

50g/2oz/¼ cup butter, softened
50g/2oz/¼ cup caster (superfine) sugar
1 egg
45g/1¾oz/scant ½ cup self-raising (self-rising) flour, sifted
15g/½oz unsweetened cocoa powder, sifted, plus extra for dusting
15ml/1 tbsp buttermilk
a few drops of red food colouring gel
20 wooden skewers

For the cream cheese icing
200g/7oz/1¾ cups icing (confectioners') sugar
50g/2oz white chocolate, melted and cooled
30g/1¼oz/scant ¼ cup cream cheese
15ml/1 tbsp buttermilk

To decorate
20 mini marshmallows (optional)

1 Preheat the oven to 180°C/350°F/Gas 4. Grease a 24-cup mini muffin tin (pan). To make the cakes, cream the butter and caster sugar together until light and fluffy, then beat in the egg.

2 Sift the flour and cocoa powder together in a separate bowl, then fold into the butter mixture with the buttermilk and a few drops of red food colouring gel (enough to colour the mixture an even reddish brown).

3 Divide the cake mixture (batter) between 20 cups of the prepared mini muffin tin. Bake for 12–15 minutes, or until the cakes spring back when gently pressed. Transfer to a wire rack to cool.

4 For the icing, sift the icing sugar into a bowl, add the white chocolate, cream cheese and buttermilk, and whisk for 3 minutes, or until creamy.

5 Using a piping (pastry) bag fitted with a large star-shaped nozzle, pipe a swirl of icing on top of each cake. Dust with a little sifted cocoa powder and, when ready to serve, insert a wooden skewer into the base of each cake, securing with a mini marshmallow, if necessary.

Energy 103kcal/433 kJ; Protein 1g; Carbohydrate 16g, of which sugars 15g; Fat 4g, of which saturates 2g; Cholesterol 20mg; Calcium 22mg; Fibre 0.1g; Sodium 44mg.

Mini Cupcake Pops

Classic cake pops, these dainty mini cakes are ideal for parties. Decorated with icing (which you could colour, if you like) and pretty sugar sprinkles, your guests will not be able to resist their cuteness. Use different coloured cake cases to add some variety.

Makes 24

115g/4oz/½ cup butter, softened
115g/4oz/generous ½ cup caster
  (superfine) sugar
2 eggs
75g/3oz/⅔ cup self-raising
  (self-rising) flour
25g/1oz unsweetened cocoa
  powder
15ml/1 tbsp natural (plain) yogurt
24 wooden skewers

For the buttercream icing
200g/7oz/1¾ cups icing
  (confectioners') sugar
50g/2oz/¼ cup butter, softened
15–30ml/1–2 tbsp milk

To decorate
coloured sugar sprinkles

1 Preheat the oven to 180°C/350°F/Gas 4. Place mini paper cake cases in a 24-cup mini muffin tin (pan). To make the cakes, cream the butter and sugar together until light and fluffy. Beat in the eggs.

2 Sift the flour and cocoa powder into the butter mixture, then fold in with the yogurt. Divide the cake mixture (batter) between the cases; about a heaped teaspoonful in each.

3 Bake for 12–15 minutes, until the cakes spring back when pressed. Transfer to a wire rack to cool.

4 To prepare the icing, sift the icing sugar into a bowl, add the butter and half of the milk. Whisk together for 3 minutes, until light and creamy, adding more milk if necessary.

5 Spoon the icing into a piping (pastry) bag fitted with a large star-shaped nozzle, and pipe a swirl of icing on top of each cupcake. Decorate with sugar sprinkles.

6 Insert a wooden skewer into the base of each cake and display for serving. Depending on the thickness of your cake cases, you may need to pierce the paper cases with a sharp knife before inserting the skewers.

Energy 125kcal/526 kJ; Protein 1g; Carbohydrate 16g, of which sugars 14g; Fat 7g, of which saturates 4g; Cholesterol 34mg; Calcium 21mg; Fibre 0.1g; Sodium 73mg.

Banana Cake Pops

These little cakes take their inspiration from the ever-popular banoffee pie, packed with ripe bananas and a buttery caramel sauce. Topped with a crunchy banana chip, they are sure to be a hit. The lemon juice is added to the mashed banana to prevent it from discolouring.

Makes 24

1 banana, peeled
juice of 1 lemon
50g/2oz/¼ cup butter, softened
50g/2oz/4 tbsp soft light brown
  sugar
1 egg
50g/2oz/½ cup self-raising
  (self-rising) flour
15ml/1 tbsp buttermilk
30g/1¼ oz/scant ¼ cup sultanas
  (golden raisins)
24 wooden skewers, to serve
For the toffee glaze
65g/2½oz/5 tbsp soft dark
  brown sugar
65g/2½oz/5 tbsp butter
45ml/3 tbsp maple syrup
30ml/2 tbsp double (heavy)
  cream
To decorate
24 banana chips

1 Preheat the oven to 180°C/350°F/Gas 4. Grease a 24-cup mini muffin tin (pan).

2 For the cakes, mash the banana and lemon juice together using a fork until you have a paste. Cream the butter and sugar together in a separate bowl until light and fluffy. Beat in the egg and banana paste.

3 Sift in the flour and fold in with the buttermilk and sultanas.

4 Divide the cake mixture (batter) between the cups of the prepared mini muffin tin. Bake for 12–15 minutes, or until the cakes spring back when pressed. Transfer to a wire rack to cool.

5 For the toffee glaze, place the sugar, butter and maple syrup in a pan and simmer over a gentle heat until the sugar has dissolved. Add the cream and whisk over the heat for a few minutes. Remove from the heat.

6 Invert the cakes so they are wider at the bottom than at the top. Press a banana chip into the top of each.

7 Coat each cake with the toffee glaze using a spoon. Insert a wooden skewer into the base of each cake and serve immediately.

Energy 82kcal/341kJ; Protein 0g; Carbohydrate 9g, of which sugars 8g; Fat 5g, of which saturates 3g; Cholesterol 22mg; Calcium 21mg; Fibre 0.3g; Sodium 49mg.

Whoopie Pie Pops

An American favourite, whoopie pies are said to have been given their name by Amish farmers who would whoop with delight when they found them in their lunch packs. They are best eaten fresh, so serve them on the day they are made.

Makes 30

125g/4¼oz/8½ tbsp butter, softened
200g/7oz/1 cup caster (superfine) sugar
1 egg
5ml/1 tsp vanilla extract
325g/11½oz/scant 3 cups self-raising (self-rising) flour
5ml/1 tsp baking powder
250ml/8fl oz/1 cup buttermilk
100ml/3½fl oz/scant ½ cup hot water
a few drops of pink and green food colouring gels
30 short wooden skewers

For the chocolate cream filling

225ml/7½fl oz/scant 1 cup double (heavy) cream
300g/11oz white chocolate, melted and cooled

1 First, make the filling, as this needs to set in the refrigerator to be thick enough to hold the pops on the skewers. Whip the cream to stiff peaks. Fold in the melted chocolate and chill for 30 minutes, or until needed.

2 Preheat the oven to 180°C/350°F/Gas 4. Grease and line two baking sheets with baking parchment or silicone mats. For the cakes, cream the butter and sugar together for 2–3 minutes, until light and creamy. Whisk in the egg and vanilla extract.

3 Sift the flour and baking powder into the bowl and add the buttermilk. Whisk again. The mixture will be quite stiff. Whisk in the hot water. Divide the cake mixture (batter) into two bowls. Stir the pink food colouring gel into one bowl of the mixture and the green food colouring gel into the other.

4 Using two piping (pastry) bags fitted with large plain nozzles, pipe 30 2.5cm/1in rounds of each mixture on to each baking sheet, making 60 cakes. Bake for 10–12 minutes, or until they are firm to touch. Transfer to a wire rack to cool.

5 Using a separate piping (pastry) bag fitted with a small star-shaped nozzle, pipe some filling on to the flat sides of half of the cakes. Top with the remaining cakes. Leave to set, then poke skewers into the filling of each pie to serve.

Energy 192kcal/806 kJ; Protein 3g; Carbohydrate 22g, of which sugars 14g; Fat 11g, of which saturates 7g; Cholesterol 27mg; Calcium 86mg; Fibre 0.5g; Sodium 108mg.

Coconut Ice Pops

Long, soft shredded coconut looks very pretty when coloured, and has a wide number of uses in baking. Fondant icing sugar is used for the icing. It contains glucose syrup to give it an attractive sheen and is ideal for icing mini cakes.

Makes 20

50g/2oz/¼ cup butter, softened
50g/2oz/¼ cup caster
   (superfine) sugar
1 egg
50g/2oz/½ cup self-raising
   (self-rising) flour
15ml/1 tbsp natural (plain) yogurt
30g/1¼oz desiccated (dry
   unsweetened shredded)
   coconut
20 small wooden skewers

For the coconut topping and icing
65g/2½oz long soft shredded
   coconut
a few drops of pink food
   colouring gel
100g/3¾oz/scant 1 cup fondant
   icing sugar or icing
   (confectioners') sugar
15–30ml/1–2 tbsp water

To decorate
edible glitter

1 Preheat the oven to 180°C/350°F/Gas 4. Grease a 20-hole mini loaf silicone mould.

2 For the cakes, cream the butter and caster sugar together until light and fluffy. Beat in the egg. Sift the flour into the butter mixture and fold in with the yogurt and coconut. Divide the cake mixture (batter) between the holes of the prepared mould.

3 Bake for 15–18 minutes, or until the cakes spring back when pressed. Transfer to a wire rack to cool.

4 To make the topping, put half of the coconut in a bowl, add a few drops of pink food colouring gel and stir until it is evenly coloured. Add the remaining white coconut to the pink coconut and mix. Set aside.

5 For the icing, sift the fondant icing sugar into a bowl, add the water and mix to a smooth icing, adding a little extra if necessary.

6 To decorate, insert a wooden skewer into one of the short ends of each cake. Partly cover each cake with a little of the icing. Place the iced cakes on a wire rack, sprinkle over the mixed pink and white coconut, then sprinkle with some edible glitter. Let the icing set before serving.

Energy 82kcal/342kJ; Protein 1g; Carbohydrate 10g, of which sugars 8g; Fat 5g, of which saturates 3g; Cholesterol 17mg; Calcium 12mg; Fibre 0.8g; Sodium 31mg.

Polka Dot Cookie Pops

Cookie pops are really just an excuse to have an extra-large cookie! These pops look very pretty decorated with coloured candy-coated chocolates. They would be a perfect treat to hide in children's party bags, sure to put a smile on their faces when they discover them.

Makes 10

325g/11½oz/scant 3 cups plain (all-purpose) flour

30g/1¼oz unsweetened cocoa powder

5ml/1 tsp bicarbonate of soda (baking soda)

125g/4¼oz/8½ tbsp butter

45ml/3 tbsp golden (light corn) syrup

90g/3½oz/scant ½ cup cream cheese

1 egg, beaten

100g/3¾oz plain (semisweet) chocolate chips

about 60 candy-coated chocolates

10 ice lolly (popsicle) sticks

1 Preheat the oven to 180°C/350°F/Gas 4. Grease and line two large baking sheets.

2 Sift the flour, cocoa powder and bicarbonate of soda into a bowl.

3 Put the butter and syrup in a pan and heat gently until melted and evenly blended. Remove from the heat and allow to cool slightly, then stir into the dry ingredients using a wooden spoon.

4 Beat in the cream cheese, egg and chocolate chips to make a dough. Divide the dough into 10 equal portions and roll each one into a small ball. Place the balls of dough on the prepared baking sheets, leaving a gap between each one as they will spread during cooking.

5 Press each ball flat using your fingertips, then gently press five or six candy-coated chocolates on to the top of each cookie. Insert an ice lolly stick into the side of each cookie, ensuring that the top of the stick is completely covered in cookie dough.

6 Bake for 12–15 minutes, or until the cookies are just firm. Allow the cookies to cool on the baking sheets for 5 minutes, then transfer them to a wire rack to cool completely.

Energy 268kcal/1127 kJ; Protein 6g; Carbohydrate 13g, of which sugars 7g; Fat 6g, of which saturates 4g; Cholesterol 34mg; Calcium 34mg; Fibre 0.4g; Sodium 76mg.

Swirly Pops

These brightly coloured cookie pops are decorated to look like traditional candy lollipops. They would be perfect for a Willy Wonka-themed party. You can use any colour icing you like – green and red for Christmas, or the colour of the child's team for a sports party.

Makes 8

115g/4oz/½ cup butter, softened
50g/2oz/¼ cup caster
  (superfine) sugar
175g/6oz/1½ cups plain
  (all-purpose) flour, sifted,
  plus extra for dusting
5ml/1 tsp vanilla extract
15ml/1 tbsp milk, to mix
  (optional)
8 ice lolly (popsicle) sticks

For the pink icing
250g/9oz/2¼ cups royal icing
  sugar (*see page* 11), sifted
15ml/1 tbsp water
a few drops of pink food
  colouring gel

For the white icing
100g/3¾oz/scant 1 cup fondant
  (regal) icing sugar (*see page*
  11), sifted
5ml/1 tsp vanilla extract
15–25ml/1–1½ tbsp water

To decorate
pink and white sugar sprinkles

1 To make the cookies, whisk the butter and caster sugar together until pale and creamy.

2 Sift the flour into the bowl, add the vanilla extract and mix to form a soft dough. If the mixture is too dry, blend in the milk. Wrap the dough in clear film (plastic wrap) and chill for about 1 hour. Meanwhile, preheat the oven to 180°C/350°F/Gas 4. Grease and line two large baking sheets.

3 On a lightly floured surface, roll out the dough to a thickness of 1cm/½in. Cut out 8 rounds using a 7.5cm/3in round pastry (cookie) cutter. Place the cookies on the baking sheets and insert an ice lolly stick into the base of each cookie. Ensure that the top of the stick is completely covered in dough.

4 Bake for 10–15 minutes, or until golden. Leave to cool on the baking sheets for 5 minutes, then transfer to a wire rack to cool completely.

5 For the pink icing, put the royal icing sugar in a bowl with the water and pink food colouring gel. Whisk until the icing is smooth (this will take about 5 minutes). Using a piping (pastry) bag fitted with a small plain nozzle, pipe a spiral of pink icing on to the top of each cookie. Allow the pink icing to set.

6 For the white icing, put the fondant icing sugar into a bowl and stir in the vanilla extract and enough water to make a smooth icing. Using another piping bag fitted with a small plain nozzle, pipe in a spiral pattern between the lines of pink icing.

7 Shake the cookies slightly so that the white icing spreads to completely fill the holes between the pink icing. Decorate with sugar sprinkles, then leave to set before serving.

Energy 368kcal/1529 kJ; Protein 3g; Carbohydrate 65g, of which sugars 48g; Fat 12g, of which saturates 8g; Cholesterol 31mg; Calcium 38mg; Fibre 0.8g; Sodium 102mg.

Millionaire's Shortbread Pops

The perfectly combined teatime snack, millionaire's shortbread comprises rich chocolate, sticky caramel and buttery shortbread. These little pop versions would make a popular after-school treat, and the stick means that you get to keep your fingers clean while you eat them.

Makes 12

115g/4oz/½ cup butter, softened
50g/2oz/¼ cup caster (superfine) sugar
175g/6oz/1½ cups plain (all-purpose) flour, plus extra for dusting
5ml/1 tsp vanilla extract
15ml/1 tbsp milk, to mix (optional)
12 ice lolly (popsicle) sticks

For the caramel

150g/5oz/¾ cup caster (superfine) sugar
50g/2oz/¼ cup butter
45ml/3 tbsp double (heavy) cream

To decorate

100g/3¾oz milk chocolate, melted
coloured sugar sprinkles

1 To make the shortbread, whisk the butter and caster sugar together until pale and creamy.

2 Sift the flour into the bowl, add the vanilla extract and mix to a soft dough. If the mixture is too dry, add in the milk. Wrap the dough in clear film (plastic wrap). Chill for 1 hour. Preheat the oven to 180°C/350°F/Gas 4. Grease and line two baking sheets.

3 On a lightly floured surface, roll out the dough to 1cm/½in thickness. Cut into 12 rectangular cookies. Arrange the cookies on the baking sheets. Insert a stick into the base of each one, ensuring that the top of the stick is completely covered in dough.

4 Bake for 12–15 minutes, or until golden. Leave the cookies to cool completely on the baking sheets. Once cool, transfer them to a wire rack.

5 To make the caramel, put the caster sugar and butter in a pan and simmer over a gentle heat until the sugar has dissolved and the mixture has turned golden brown. Add the cream and stir over the heat for a few minutes more.

6 Remove from the heat and leave the caramel to cool for 5 minutes. Place a sheet of foil or baking parchment under the wire rack to collect the drips. Dip each cookie into the caramel to coat all over, then place them back on the wire rack to set.

7 To decorate, dip the caramel-coated cookies in the melted chocolate. Decorate with sugar sprinkles and leave to set before serving.

Energy 244kcal/1020kJ; Protein 3g; Carbohydrate 25g, of which sugars 14g; Fat 15g, of which saturates 3g; Cholesterol 35mg; Calcium 68mg; Fibre 0.5g; Sodium 114mg.

Meringue Pops

These dainty pink meringues are the lightest of treats and are perfect for an afternoon tea party. They are filled with a rich and creamy chocolate ganache. Make sure that the meringues are small enough to be just one mouthful.

Makes 20

3 egg whites
175g/6oz/scant 1 cup caster (superfine) sugar
5ml/1 tsp vanilla extract
a few drops of pink food colouring gel
20 cocktail sticks (toothpicks)
For the chocolate ganache
100g/3¾oz plain (semisweet) chocolate, roughly chopped
15g/½oz/1 tbsp butter
50ml/2fl oz/¼ cup double (heavy) cream

Variation

If you prefer, replace the chocolate ganache with raspberry jam and buttercream.

1 Preheat the oven to 140°C/275°F/Gas 1. Line two baking sheets with silicone mats or grease and line with baking parchment.

2 For the meringues, place the egg whites and caster sugar in a heatproof bowl set over a pan of simmering water. It is important that the bottom of the bowl does not touch the water. Using an electric whisk, whisk the egg whites and sugar together over the heat for 5 minutes, or until they are foamy. Remove the bowl from the heat and whisk the mixture for 5 minutes more, or until the meringue is stiff. Fold in the vanilla extract and food colouring.

3 Using a piping (pastry) bag fitted with a large plain nozzle, pipe 40 rounds of meringue on to the prepared baking sheets.

4 Bake for 1–1¼ hours, or until the meringues are dried and crisp. Leave the meringues to cool completely on the baking sheets.

5 To make the chocolate ganache, place the chocolate, butter and cream in a separate heatproof bowl set over a pan of simmering water, taking care that the bottom of the bowl does not touch the water. Stir until the chocolate has melted and the mixture is smooth and glossy, then remove from the heat and leave to cool for approximately 1 hour, or until thickened.

6 Using a piping bag fitted with a plain nozzle, pipe a round of ganache on to the flat side of half of the meringues. Top with the flat sides of the remaining meringue halves. Allow to set. Press a cocktail stick into the filling to serve.

Energy 80kcal/335 kJ; Protein 1g; Carbohydrate 12g, of which sugars 12g; Fat 3g, of which saturates 2g; Cholesterol 5mg; Calcium 4mg; Fibre 0g; Sodium 15mg.

Honey Bee Pops

These honey-flavoured buzzy little bees with edible rice paper wings are perfect for a teddy bear's picnic or doll's tea party. With honey-infused sponge, enrobed in creamy white chocolate, the little pops taste delicious and look as pretty as a picture.

Makes 28

80g/3¼oz/6½ tbsp butter, softened
30ml/2 tbsp clear honey
50g/2oz/¼ cup caster (superfine) sugar
1 egg
50g/2oz/½ cup self-raising (self-rising) flour
15ml/1 tbsp buttermilk
100g/3¾oz/scant ½ cup cream cheese
28 lollipop sticks

To decorate

a few drops of yellow food colouring gel
200g/7oz white chocolate, melted
45ml/3 tbsp icing (confectioners') sugar
a few drops of black food colouring gel
a few teaspoons of warm water
8 small sheets of edible rice paper

1 Preheat the oven to 180°C/350°F/Gas 4. Grease and line a 20cm/8in square cake tin (pan).

2 To make the cakes, cream 50g/2oz/¼ cup butter, 15ml/1 tbsp of the honey and the caster sugar together until light and fluffy. Beat in the egg. Sift the flour into the butter mixture, add the buttermilk and fold in. Spoon the cake mixture (batter) into the cake tin and level the surface.

3 Bake for 15–20 minutes, or until the cake is golden brown, springs back when gently pressed and the tip of a sharp knife comes out clean when inserted into the centre. Leave to cool in the tin for a couple of minutes, then turn the cake on to a wire rack to cool completely.

4 When the cake is cool, process it to crumbs in a food processor.

5 Transfer the cake crumbs to a bowl, add the cream cheese, the remaining 30g/1¼oz/2½ tbsp butter and 15ml/1 tbsp honey. Mix together.

6 Shape the mixture into 28 egg-shaped balls, each about 1½cm/⅝in diameter. Place the balls on a tray and chill in the freezer for 30 minutes.

7 Press a stick into each egg-shape. To decorate, whisk a few drops of yellow food colouring gel into the melted white chocolate, then dip each pop into it, coating all over. Press the stick into a foam block. Leave to set.

8 In a separate bowl, mix together the icing sugar, black food colouring gel and enough warm water to make a thick, stiff icing. Using a piping (pastry) bag fitted with a small plain nozzle, pipe thin black lines on to each cake pop for the bee's stripes, then add two small dots for eyes.

9 Cut the rice paper into small wing shapes, each about 2cm/¾in long, then press on to the cake pops using a little of the melted yellow chocolate. Leave to set, then chill until ready to serve.

Energy 95kcal/408 kJ; Protein 1g; Carbohydrate 12g, of which sugars 12g; Fat 5g, of which saturates 1g; Cholesterol 14mg; Calcium 10mg; Fibre 0.2g; Sodium 40mg.

Fairy Wand Pops

You can make these into any shape you wish, or cut them into round shapes and fill with peppermint dust to make magnifying glasses. Silicone mats are ideal as the sugar glass does not stick to it. If you do not have these, grease the baking sheets with flavourless oil.

Makes 6

12 cola-flavoured boiled sweets (hard candies)
115g/4oz/½ cup butter, softened
50g/2oz/¼ cup caster (superfine) sugar
5ml/1 tsp vanilla extract
175g/6oz/1½ cups plain (all-purpose) flour, plus extra for dusting
15ml/1 tbsp milk, to mix (optional)

For the icing and decoration

100g/3¾oz/scant 1 cup fondant (regal) icing sugar (*see page 11*)
15–30ml/1–2 tbsp water
a few drops of pink food colouring gel
mini marshmallows
edible silver balls
edible glitter, for sprinkling

1   For the cookies, remove any wrappers from the sweets and blitz them to a fine dust in a blender or food processor. Set aside.

2   Using an electric hand mixer or whisk, whisk the butter, sugar and vanilla extract together until pale and creamy. Sift the flour into the bowl and stir in to form a soft dough. If the mixture is too dry, stir in a little milk. Wrap the dough in clear film (plastic wrap) and chill in the refrigerator for about 1 hour.

3   Preheat the oven to 180°C/350°F/Gas 4. Place silicone mats on two baking sheets. On a lightly floured surface, roll out the dough to a thickness of 8mm/⅜in. Cut out 6 wand shapes using a card template

4   Carefully transfer the wands to the prepared baking sheets. Use a small star cutter to cut out a star from the centre of the top of each wand. Fill the hole with a little of the cola dust.

5   Bake for 12–15 minutes, or until the wands are golden and the cola crystals have all melted. Leave to cool completely on the baking sheets so that the sugar glass solidifies.

6   For the icing, sift the fondant icing sugar into a bowl and stir in enough water to give a smooth, thick icing. Stir in the pink food colouring gel.

7   Using a piping (pastry) bag fitted with a tiny plain nozzle, pipe lines of icing around the wands. Decorate with the marshmallows, silver balls and glitter. Leave to set before serving.

Energy 401kcal/1687kJ; Protein 3g; Carbohydrate 64g, of which sugars 41g; Fat 16g, of which saturates 10g; Cholesterol 41mg; Calcium 51mg; Fibre 1.1g; Sodium 129mg.

Frog Pops

These cute little frog pops are as green as can be, with bright green cake inside and a green chocolate coating. If you are having a scary monster party, you could change the colour of the chocolate to blue or red and pipe wiggly lines of icing for mouths.

Makes 30

80g/3¼oz/6½ tbsp butter, softened
50g/2oz/¼ cup caster (superfine) sugar
1 egg
50g/2oz/½ cup self-raising (self-rising) flour
15ml/1 tbsp buttermilk
a few drops of green food colouring gel
100g/3¾oz/scant ½ cup cream cheese
30 lollipop sticks

For the decoration
a few drops of green food colouring gel
200g/7oz white chocolate, melted
60 green mini candy-coated chocolates

For the icing
50g/2oz/½ cup icing (confectioners') sugar
25g/1oz/2 tbsp butter, softened
5ml/1 tsp milk, to mix (optional)
a few drops of black food colouring gel

1   Preheat the oven to 180°C/350°F/Gas 4. Grease and line a 20cm/8in square cake tin (pan). For the cakes, cream 50g/2oz/4 tbsp of the butter and the sugar together until light and fluffy. Beat in the egg. Sift in the flour and fold in with the buttermilk and green food colouring gel.

2   Spoon the mixture into the cake tin and level the surface. Bake for 15–20 minutes, until a knife inserted into the centre comes out clean. Leave for a few minutes in the tin, then transfer to a wire rack to cool.

3   Process the cake to crumbs in a food processor. Transfer the cake crumbs to a bowl, and mix in the cream cheese and the remaining 30g/1¼oz/2½ tbsp butter.

4   Shape the mixture into 30 1½cm/⅝in balls. Flatten one side of each ball where the mouth will be. Chill in the freezer for 30 minutes.

5   Press a stick into the base of each ball. To decorate, stir the green food colouring gel into the melted white chocolate. Dip in each pop, coating all over, then press the stick into a foam block and leave to set.

6   Fix two green mini candies on top of each frog just after dipping, when the green chocolate has not yet set. Use a brush to coat the candies in the melted chocolate. Add a mouth line using a cocktail stick (toothpick).

7   To prepare the icing, sift the icing sugar into a bowl, add the butter and whisk until light and creamy, adding the milk, if necessary. Transfer 15ml/1 tbsp of the icing to a separate bowl and colour this black with the black food colouring gel.

8   Spoon the two icings into separate piping (pastry) bags, both fitted with a tiny plain nozzle. Pipe small white eyes on the candies then pipe a small black dot on top for the pupils. Allow to set completely before serving.

Energy 91kcal/379kJ; Protein 1g; Carbohydrate 7g, of which sugars 6g; Fat 7g, of which saturates 4g; Cholesterol 18mg; Calcium 29mg; Fibre 0.1g; Sodium 47mg.

Rocky Road Pops

These pops take their inspiration from rocky road ice cream and are packed with cherries, chocolate and marshmallows. A crunch of two types of cookies is added for an extra treat. You will only need to cut small squares of this slice for each pop as the mixture is very rich..

Makes 28

400g/14oz plain (semisweet) chocolate, chopped
125g/4¼oz/8½ tbsp butter
100g/3¾oz/scant 2 cups digestive biscuits (graham crackers), crushed
100g/3¾oz/scant 2 cups chocolate sandwich cookies, crushed
75g/3oz mini marshmallows
150g/5oz/scant ¾ cup glacé (candied) cherries, halved
28 wooden skewers

For the topping
100g/3¾oz/scant ½ cup glacé (candied) cherries, halved
50g/2oz mini marshmallows
100g/3¾oz white chocolate, melted

1 Grease and line a 28 x 18cm/11 x 7in deep rectangular cake tin (pan).
2 To make the chocolate slice, place the chocolate and butter in a large heatproof bowl set over a pan of simmering water, taking care that the water does not touch the bottom of the bowl. Stir until the butter and chocolate are melted and blended, then remove from the heat.
3 Add all the remaining ingredients for the chocolate slice to the bowl and mix well to coat everything in the chocolate.
4 Spoon the mixture into the tin and press out flat using a spoon.
5 For the topping, sprinkle the glacé cherries and mini marshmallows over the top. Drizzle over the white chocolate in thin lines using a spoon. Leave to set in the refrigerator.
6 To serve, remove the slice from the tin and cut into 28 squares. Insert a wooden skewer into each square.

Energy 196kcal/821kJ; Protein 2g; Carbohydrate 26g, of which sugars 22g; Fat 10g, of which saturates 6g; Cholesterol 14mg; Calcium 27mg; Fibre 0.3g; Sodium 62mg.

Peanut Butter Pops

The combination of peanut butter and chocolate is a match made in heaven – the salty peanut and smooth chocolate just melt in the mouth. Here, a peanut butter sponge is coated in melted chocolate and topped with chopped honey-roasted peanuts.

Makes 28

50g/2oz/¼ cup butter, softened
50g/2oz/¼ cup caster
  (superfine) sugar
45ml/3 tbsp peanut butter
1 egg
50g/2oz/½ cup self-raising
  (self-rising) flour
100g/3¾oz/scant ½ cup cream
  cheese
50g/2oz plain (semisweet)
  chocolate chips
28 wooden skewers

To decorate

300g/11oz plain (semisweet)
  chocolate, melted
75g/3oz/¾ cup honey-roasted
  peanuts, finely chopped

Cook's Tip
A foam block is a useful way to store cake pops in the refrigerator.

1 Preheat the oven to 180°C/350°F/Gas 4. Grease and line a 20cm/8in square cake tin (pan).

2 For the cakes, cream the butter, caster sugar and 25ml/1½ tbsp of the peanut butter together in a bowl until light and fluffy. Beat in the egg.

3 Sift the flour into the bowl and fold into the butter mixture. Spoon the cake mixture (batter) into the prepared tin and level the surface.

4 Bake for 15–20 minutes, until the cake is golden and the tip of a sharp knife comes out clean when inserted into the centre of the cake. Turn out on to a wire rack to cool.

5 Process the cooled cake to crumbs in a food processor. Transfer the cake crumbs to a bowl, add the remaining peanut butter, the cream cheese and chocolate chips and mix together.

6 Shape the mixture into 28 even-sized balls. Place the balls on a tray and chill in the freezer for 30 minutes. Remove the balls from the freezer and press a wooden skewer into each one.

7 To decorate, dip each ball into the melted chocolate, then dip the tops into the chopped peanuts. Chill until you are ready to serve.

Energy 127kcal/529kJ; Protein 2g; Carbohydrate 11g, of which sugars 10g; Fat 9g, of which saturates 5g; Cholesterol 16mg; Calcium 11mg; Fibre 0.3g; Sodium 31mg.

Birthday Cake Pops

These charming little cakes, holding mini candles, make an unusual centrepiece for a birthday celebration. Topped with purple icing, vanilla buttercream and sprinkles, they look almost too pretty to eat. You can also add extra party decorations, if you like.

Makes 10

50g/2oz/¼ cup butter, softened
50g/2oz/¼ cup caster
   (superfine) sugar
1 egg
50g/2oz/½ cup self-raising
   (self-rising) flour
5ml/1 tsp vanilla extract
15ml/1 tbsp sour cream
10 wooden skewers
For the fondant icing
200g/7oz/1¾ cups fondant
   (regal) icing sugar, sifted (*see
   page* 11)
45–60ml/3–4 tbsp water
a few drops of purple food
   colouring gel
For the buttercream icing
90g/3½oz/¾ cup icing
   (confectioners') sugar, sifted
30g/1¼oz/2½ tbsp butter
15ml/1 tbsp milk
To decorate
coloured sugar sprinkles
10 mini candles, cut to 1cm/½in,
   and candle holders
10 mini marshmallows

1 Preheat the oven to 180°C/350°F/Gas 4. Grease a 10-cup straight-sided mini muffin tin (pan). For the cakes, cream the butter and caster sugar together until fluffy. Beat in the egg.

2 Sift in the flour and fold in with the vanilla extract and sour cream using a spatula. Divide the mixture between the cups of the prepared tin.

3 Bake for 12–15 minutes, or until the cakes are golden brown and spring back when gently pressed. Transfer to a wire rack to cool.

4 For the fondant icing, put the fondant icing sugar and water in a bowl with the purple food colouring gel and whisk to a smooth thin icing. Place a sheet of foil underneath the wire rack. Dip each cake into the icing to coat. Return to the wire rack and leave to set.

5 For the buttercream, sift the icing sugar into a bowl, soften the butter and add it to the bowl with half of the milk. Whisk until creamy.

6 Using a piping (pastry) bag fitted with a small star-shaped nozzle, pipe a ring of stars around the top of each cake. Decorate with sugar sprinkles. Add a mini candle to the top of each cake in a candle holder. To serve, insert a skewer into the base of each cake.

Energy 223kcal/940kJ; Protein 1g; Carbohydrate 40g, of which sugars 36g; Fat 8g, of which saturates 5g; Cholesterol 41mg; Calcium 22mg; Fibre 0.2g; Sodium 80mg.

Chocolate Mud Pie Pops

These little pops are inspired by the classic chocolate dessert, Mississippi Mud Pie – chocolate sponge, chocolate ganache and chocolate mousse. This recipe contains no fewer than six different types of chocolate, including the cocoa powder and chocolate curls.

Makes 28

50g/2oz/¼ cup butter, softened
50g/2oz/¼ cup caster (superfine) sugar
1 egg
50g/2oz/½ cup self-raising (self-rising) flour
15ml/1 tbsp unsweetened cocoa powder
100g/3¾oz/½ cup cream cheese
100g/3¾oz milk chocolate, melted
28 lollipop sticks

For the chocolate mousse
200ml/7fl oz/ 1 cup double (heavy) cream
50g/2oz nougat-chocolate (ie Toblerone or similar) melted
50g/2oz milk chocolate, melted

For the chocolate coating
100g/3¾oz white chocolate, melted
100g/3¾oz plain (semisweet) chocolate, melted

1 Preheat the oven to 180°C/350°F/Gas 4. Grease and line a 20cm/8in square cake tin (pan).

2 For the cake, cream the butter and sugar together until light and fluffy. Beat in the egg. Sift in the flour and cocoa powder, then fold in with a spatula. Spoon the mixture into the cake tin and level the surface.

3 Bake for 15–20 minutes, or until the cake springs back when pressed and the tip of a sharp knife comes out clean when inserted into the centre. Turn the cake out on to a wire rack to cool.

4 Process the cake to crumbs in a food processor. Transfer the cake crumbs to a bowl, add the cream cheese and melted chocolate and mix together.

5 Shape the mixture into 28 even-sized balls, place them on a tray and chill in the freezer for 30 minutes.

6 Meanwhile, prepare the chocolate mousse. Whip the cream to stiff peaks. Allow the melted chocolates to cool, then fold them in until you have a smooth mousse. Chill for 1 hour.

7 Press a stick into each ball. For the coating, dip half of the balls into the melted white chocolate and half into the plain chocolate. Press the sticks into a foam block and leave to set, then chill until ready to serve.

8 Just before serving, using a piping (pastry) bag fitted with a large star-shaped nozzle, pipe a star of mousse on to each pop.

Energy 102kcal/424 kJ; Protein 1g; Carbohydrate 10g, of which sugars 8g; Fat 7g, of which saturates 4g; Cholesterol 17mg; Calcium 31mg; Fibre 0.1g; Sodium 41mg.

Mocha Gold Leaf Pops

These rich mocha chocolate pops, with hints of coffee and toffee, are the ultimate truffle delight, enrobed in a chocolate ganache and topped with glinting edible gold leaf. They add a touch of luxury, and the sprinkle of edible glitter finishes them off perfectly.

Makes 30

75g/3oz/6 tbsp butter, softened
50g/2oz/¼ cup caster (superfine) sugar
1 egg
40g/1½oz/⅓ cup self-raising (self-rising) flour
15g/½oz unsweetened cocoa powder
15ml/1 tbsp coffee liqueur
15ml/1 tbsp shop-bought toffee sauce, or *see recipe* for toffee glaze, page 20
60g/2¼oz/generous ¼ cup cream cheese
30 lollipop sticks

For the chocolate ganache
200g/7oz dark (bittersweet) chocolate, chopped
105ml/7 tbsp double (heavy) cream
25g/1oz/2 tbsp butter, softened

To decorate
edible gold leaf and edible glitter

1 Preheat the oven to 180°C/350°F/Gas 4. Grease and line a 20cm/8in square cake tin (pan). For the cake, cream 50g/2oz/4 tbsp of the butter and the sugar together until light and fluffy. Beat in the egg. Sift in the flour and cocoa powder and fold into the butter mixture.

2 Spoon the cake mixture (batter) into the tin and level the surface. Bake for 15–20 minutes, until the cake springs back when pressed and the tip of a sharp knife comes out clean when inserted into the centre. Turn out on to a wire rack to cool.

3 Process the cooled cake to crumbs in a food processor.

4 Transfer the crumbs to a bowl, add the coffee liqueur, toffee sauce, the 25g/1oz/2 tbsp butter and the cream cheese, and mix together. Shape the mixture into 30 balls, each about 2cm/¾in in diameter. Place them on a tray. Chill in the freezer for 30 minutes.

5 For the ganache, place the chocolate, cream and butter in a heatproof bowl set over a pan of simmering water, taking care that the water does not touch the bottom of the bowl. Stir until you have a smooth, glossy sauce.

6 Press a stick into each ball, then dip each ball into the ganache, coating all over. Press the sticks into a foam block. Add a little edible gold leaf to the top of each pop before the ganache sets and sprinkle with edible glitter. Chill until ready to serve.

Energy 108kcal/448kJ; Protein 1g; Carbohydrate 7g, of which sugars 6g; Fat 9g, of which saturates 5g; Cholesterol 24mg; Calcium 13mg; Fibre 0.1g; Sodium 46mg.

Amaretto Pops

Chocolate and amaretto is a decadent flavour combination. These truffles are perfect for winter celebrations served with a cup of strong coffee. Enrobed in a white chocolate case and topped with crushed amaretti, they are naughty but nice treats for a special occasion.

Makes 26

120ml/4fl oz/½ cup double (heavy) cream
15ml/1 tbsp amaretto liqueur
30g/1¼oz/2½ tbsp caster (superfine) sugar
200g/7oz plain (semisweet) chocolate, chopped
50g/2oz/¼ cup butter, melted and cooled
200g/7oz white chocolate, melted
20g/¾oz amaretti, crushed
26 wooden skewers, to serve

Cook's Tip
It is important to work quickly when handling ganache as the heat from your hands may cause it to start to melt.

1 Place the cream, amaretto liqueur and sugar in a pan and simmer over a gentle heat until the sugar has dissolved, stirring occasionally.

2 Remove from the heat, add the plain chocolate and stir until melted. Beat in the melted butter.

3 Pour the mixture into a shallow tray and chill in the refrigerator for 45–60 minutes, by which time the chocolate ganache will be thick and softly set.

4 Take teaspoonfuls of the ganache and shape them into balls in your hands. Place them on to a silicone mat or a chilled plate. Return to the refrigerator and chill for a further 1 hour, or until the truffles are set.

5 Using a dipping fork, dip each truffle into the melted white chocolate, coating all over. Tap on the side of the bowl to remove any excess chocolate, then place on a wire rack to set.

6 Using a fork, drizzle a pattern of melted white chocolate on the tops, then sprinkle each truffle with crushed amaretti. Chill until set.

7 Carefully remove the truffles from the wire rack using a sharp knife and insert a skewer into the base of each one. Chill until ready to serve.

Energy 127kcal/528kJ; Protein 1g; Carbohydrate 11g, of which sugars 11g; Fat 9g, of which saturates 5g; Cholesterol 11mg; Calcium 11mg; Fibre 0g; Sodium 22mg.

Chocolate Chilli Pops

Chilli may seem an odd accompaniment to chocolate, but it really enhances the flavour of the cocoa powder. Bars of chilli-flavoured chocolate are available in most supermarkets. If you can find red lollipop sticks that are suitable for food use, all the better.

Makes 40

50g/2oz/¼ cup butter, softened
50g/2oz/¼ cup caster (superfine) sugar
1 egg
40g/1½oz/⅓ cup self-raising (self-rising) flour
25g/1oz unsweetened cocoa powder
30ml/2 tbsp sour cream
40g/1½oz plain (semisweet) chilli chocolate, finely grated
40 lollipop sticks

To decorate
75g/3oz plain (semisweet) chilli chocolate, melted
red heart sprinkles

Cook's Tip
If you can't find chilli chocolate, you can use plain (semisweet) chocolate and add a pinch of hot chilli powder to the cake mixture instead.

1 Preheat the oven to 180°C/350°F/Gas 4. Grease two 20-hole mini hemispherical silicone moulds.

2 To make the cakes, cream the butter and sugar together until light and fluffy. Beat in the egg.

3 Sift in the flour and cocoa powder and fold in with the sour cream and grated chocolate. Spoon the cake mixture (batter) into the holes of the prepared moulds, dividing it evenly.

4 Bake the cakes for 10–15 minutes, or until the cakes spring back when gently pressed. Transfer to a wire rack to cool. Once cool, poke a stick into the base of each cake.

5 Press the sticks into a foam block. To decorate, drizzle the pops with melted chilli chocolate and top with red heart sprinkles. Let the chocolate set before serving.

Energy 35kcal/144kJ; Protein 0g; Carbohydrate 3g, of which sugars 3g; Fat 2g, of which saturates 1g; Cholesterol 9mg; Calcium 4mg; Fibre 0g; Sodium 16mg.

Valentine Pops

If you want to treat a loved one on Valentine's Day, bake them some of these homemade heart pops – flavoured with roses, the flower of love. These colourful cookies are decorated with sugar hearts and pretty pink icing.

Makes 8

50g/2oz/¼ cup caster (superfine) sugar
115g/4oz/½ cup butter, softened
175g/6oz/1½ cups plain (all-purpose) flour, plus extra for dusting
15ml/1 tbsp rose syrup
15ml/1 tbsp milk (optional)
8 ice lolly (popsicle) sticks
For the icing and decoration
200g/7oz/1¾ cups icing (confectioners') sugar
45–60ml/3–4 tbsp warm water
a few drops of pink food colouring gel
sugar heart sprinkles

Cook's Tip
These cookies look very pretty presented in cellophane bags, tied with ribbons to decorate.

1 For the cookies, using an electric hand mixer or whisk, whisk the sugar and butter until pale and creamy. Sift in the flour, add the rose syrup and mix together to form a soft dough. If the mixture is too dry, add the milk, mixing well. Wrap the dough in clear film (plastic wrap) and chill for 1 hour.

2 Preheat the oven to 180°C/350°F/Gas 4. Grease and line two baking sheets. On a floured surface, roll out the dough to a thickness of 8mm/⅜in. Cut out 8 heart shapes using a 10cm/4in heart-shaped cutter. Place the cookies on the prepared baking sheets and insert an ice lolly stick into the base of each cookie.

3 Bake for 10–15 minutes, or until golden brown. Leave the cookies to cool completely on the baking sheets.

4 To make the icing, sift the icing sugar into a bowl and stir in enough warm water to give a smooth, thick icing. Stir in a few drops of pink food colouring gel.

5 Spread the icing evenly over the cookies and decorate with the sugar heart sprinkles. Leave the icing to set before serving.

Energy 310kcal/1305kJ; Protein 2g; Carbohydrate 51g, of which sugars 34g; Fat 12g, of which saturates 8g; Cholesterol 31mg; Calcium 37mg; Fibre 0.8g; Sodium 97mg.

Chocolate Easter Egg Pops

These little chocolate eggs are a delightful Easter celebration – there is nothing more creative and rewarding than making your own Easter eggs! You need small plastic Easter egg moulds to make these pops. They are available from good cookshops and online.

Makes 8

200g/7oz milk or plain (semisweet) chocolate, melted
250g/9oz/2¼ cups royal icing sugar, sifted (*see page* 11)
45ml/3 tbsp water
a few drops of pink food colouring gel
8 thin wooden skewers
8 sugar flowers. to decorate

Cook's Tip

Adjust the amount of chocolate for different-sized moulds. This recipe is for moulds 6cm/2½ in in height and 3cm/1¼ in in width.

1 Pour the melted chocolate into 16 Easter egg moulds and spread out so that each mould is coated in chocolate. Leave to set for 15 minutes, then apply a second coat of chocolate to each egg mould. Chill until set.
2 Put the royal icing sugar and water in a bowl and whisk together for about 5 minutes, or until the icing is light and airy, and holds its shape when you lift the whisk up.
3 Add a few drops of pink food colouring gel and beat again.
4 Remove the chocolate moulds from the refrigerator and carefully pop the chocolate egg shells out. Trim the edges of each eggshell using a sharp knife. Touch the chocolate as little as possible to avoid fingerprints.
5 Hold two half shells together and, using a piping (pastry) bag fitted with a small star-shaped nozzle, pipe stars of icing over the join all around the egg. Pipe a small star of icing on the front of the egg and top with a sugar flower. Return to the refrigerator and repeat with all the remaining egg shells.
6 When ready to serve, carefully push a wooden skewer into the base of each egg.

Energy 250kcal/1059 kJ; Protein 1g; Carbohydrate 49g, of which sugars 48g; Fat 7g, of which saturates 4g; Cholesterol 2mg; Calcium 9mg; Fibre 0g; Sodium 5mg.

Halloween Ghost Pops

When little ghosts and ghouls come calling on All Hallows' Eve, delight them with Halloween ghost pops. To display them, why not hollow out a small pumpkin and fill with a foam block, covered with foil? Poke the sticks in and cover the foil with mini marshmallows.

Makes 24

50g/2oz/¼ cup butter, softened
50g/2oz/¼ cup caster
    (superfine) sugar
1 egg
50g/2oz/½ cup self-raising
    (self-rising) flour
15ml/1 tbsp natural (plain) yogurt
24 lollipop sticks

**For the buttercream icing and
    decoration**

200g/7oz/1¾ cups icing
    (confectioners') sugar,
    plus extra for dusting
40g/1½oz/3 tbsp butter, softened
30ml/2 tbsp milk
a few drops of black food
    colouring gel
300g/11oz ready-to-roll white
    icing (sugarpaste)

To serve

24 mini marshmallows

1 Preheat the oven to 180°C/350°F/Gas 4. Grease a 24-cup mini muffin tin (pan).

2 For the cakes, cream the butter and sugar together until light and fluffy. Beat in the egg. Sift in the flour and fold it in with the yogurt. Spoon a heaped teaspoon of cake mixture (batter) into each cup of the prepared mini muffin tin.

3 Bake for 12–15 minutes, until the cakes are golden and spring back when pressed. Transfer to a wire rack to cool.

4 To prepare the buttercream icing, sift the icing sugar into a bowl, add the butter and half of the milk. Whisk together for about 3 minutes, or until light and creamy, adding a little more milk if necessary. Reserve a heaped tablespoonful of the buttercream and colour this with a few drops of black food colouring gel. Set this aside for decoration.

5 Invert the cakes so that the smaller base of each is facing upwards. Using a round-bladed knife, cover the sides and top of each cake with white buttercream icing.

6 Roll out the ready-to-roll icing on an icing sugar-dusted surface until it is very thin.

7 Using an 8cm/3¼in round cutter, cut out 24 rounds of icing. Drape one over each cake, inserting a stick into the base of each. Secure the base with a mini marshmallow.

8 Using a piping (pastry) bag fitted with a small plain nozzle, pipe little features on each ghost, using the reserved black icing.

Energy 126kcal/532 kJ; Protein 1g; Carbohydrate 25g, of which sugars 23g; Fat 3g, of which saturates 2g; Cholesterol 18mg; Calcium 13mg; Fibre 0.1g; Sodium 40mg.

Snowmen Pops

These tiny snowmen, made from light meringues and decorated with orange noses and icing scarves, are almost too cute to eat. The meringues are quick and easy to prepare, and they keep well stored in an airtight container, so you can make ahead of time.

Makes 25

2 egg whites
115g/4oz/generous ½ cup caster (superfine) sugar
100g/3¾oz/scant 1 cup fondant (regal) icing sugar (*see page 11*)
15–30ml/1–2 tbsp water
a few drops of black, orange and blue food colouring gels
25 thin wooden skewers

Variation
For 3D scarves, use thin liquorice bootlaces, if you like.

1 Preheat the oven to 140°C/275°F/Gas 1. Line two baking sheets with silicone mats or baking parchment.
2 Place the egg whites in a bowl and whisk them until they hold stiff peaks. Gradually add the caster sugar, a tablespoonful at a time, whisking constantly until the meringue is shiny and glossy.
3 Using a piping (pastry) bag fitted with a large plain nozzle, pipe twenty-five 3cm/1¼in rounds on to the baking sheets.
4 Pipe a second, smaller round on top of each one to give a snowman shape, with a body and smaller head. Smooth the top of the second round using a finger. Bake for 1–1¼ hours, or until the meringues are dried and crisp. Leave them to cool completely on the baking sheets.
5 Sift the fondant icing sugar into a bowl and stir in enough water to give a smooth, thick icing. Divide the icing among three bowls and add black food colouring gel to one, orange to another and blue to the third.
6 Using three piping (pastry) bags, pipe an orange carrot nose, a thin blue scarf, three black buttons and two black eyes onto each snowman. Leave the icing to set then insert a wooden skewer into each one.

Energy 35kcal/148kJ; Protein 0g; Carbohydrate 9g, of which sugars 9g; Fat 0g, of which saturates 0g; Cholesterol 0mg; Calcium 1mg; Fibre 0g; Sodium 6mg.

Christmas Pudding Pops

Why not add to the Christmas festivities by making these delicious pops? Spicy sponge cake mixed with melted white chocolate and cream cheese, dipped in rich chocolate ganache and topped with white chocolate and Christmas decorations, they will delight all the family.

Makes 30

50g/2oz/¼ cup butter, softened
50g/2oz/¼ cup caster (superfine) sugar
1 egg
50g/2oz/½ cup self-raising (self-rising) flour, sifted
5ml/1 tsp ground Christmas cake spice
5ml/1 tsp ground cinnamon
100g/3¾oz white chocolate, melted
100g/3¾oz/scant ½ cup cream cheese
30 lollipop sticks

For the chocolate ganache
200g/7oz plain (semisweet) chocolate, chopped
30g/1¼oz/2½ tbsp butter
105ml/7 tbsp double (heavy) cream

To decorate
65g/2½oz white chocolate, melted
30 mini sugar holly decorations

1   Preheat the oven to 180°C/350°F/Gas 4. Grease and line a 20cm/8in square cake tin (pan).

2   For the cake, cream the butter and sugar until light and fluffy. Beat in the egg. Sift in the flour and fold in with the spices. Spoon the mixture (batter) into the cake tin and level the surface.

3   Bake for 15–20 minutes, until the cake springs back when pressed and the tip of a sharp knife comes out clean when inserted into the centre. Turn out on to a wire rack to cool.

4   Process the cooled cake to crumbs in a food processor. Transfer the crumbs to a mixing bowl, add the melted white chocolate and cream cheese, and mix together. Shape the mixture into 30 balls, 2cm/¾in in diameter. Place the balls on a tray and chill them in the freezer for 30 minutes.

5   Meanwhile, make the ganache. Place the plain chocolate, butter and double cream in a heatproof bowl set over a pan of simmering water, taking care that the water does not touch the bottom of the bowl. Stir until you have a smooth, glossy sauce. Remove the bowl from the heat and leave the ganache to cool and thicken.

6   Press a stick into each ball. Dip each ball into the chocolate ganache, coating all over. Press the wooden skewers into a foam block to secure each pop and leave to set.

7   To decorate, dip the top of each ball into the melted white chocolate, then top with a sugar holly decoration, and leave to set. Chill until ready to serve.

Energy 79kcal/328kJ; Protein 1g; Carbohydrate 7g, of which sugars 7g; Fat 6g, of which saturates 3g; Cholesterol 16mg; Calcium 22mg; Fibre 0g; Sodium 34mg.

64

Index

amaretto pops 50

banana cake pops 20
birthday cake pops 44
buttercream, preparing 10

cake pop, making 11
caramel
   millionaire's shortbread pops 32
cherries
   rocky road pops 40
chilli
   chocolate chilli pops 52
chocolate
   amaretto pops 50
   chocolate chilli pops 52
   chocolate coating 46
   chocolate Easter egg pops 56
   chocolate mud pie pops 46
   Christmas pudding pops 62
   frog pops 38
   ganache 30, 62
   honey bee pops 34
   melting 10
   meringue pops 32
   millionaire's shortbread pops 32

mini cupcake pops 18
mocha gold leaf pops 48
peanut butter pops 42
polka dot cookie pops 26
red velvet pops 16
rocky road pops 40
whoopie pie pops 22
Christmas pudding pops 62
coconut ice pops 24
coffee
   mocha gold leaf pops 48
cookies
   millionaire's shortbread pops 30
   polka dot cookie pops 26
   swirly pops 28
   Valentine pops 54
cupcake pops, mini 18

decorating 7, 11
displaying 6

Easter egg pops, chocolate 56
equipment 8

fairy wand pops 36
frog pops 38

Halloween ghost pops 58
honey bee pops 34

icing
   buttercream 18, 44, 58
   cream cheese 16
   fondant 44
   sugars 11

maple syrup
   banana cake pops 20
marshmallows
   birthday cake pops 44

fairy wand pops 36
Halloween ghost pops 58
red velvet pops 16
rocky road pops 40
meringues
   meringue pops 32
   snowmen pops 60
millionaire's shortbread pops 32
mini cupcake pops 18
mocha gold leaf pops 48

peanut butter pops 42
polka dot cookie pops 26

red velvet pops 16
rocky road pops 40

shortbread pops, millionaire's 30
snowmen pops 60
swirly pops 28

toffee glaze 20
toffee sauce
   mocha gold leaf pops 48

Valentine pops 54
Victoria sponge pops, mini 14

whoopie pie pops 22